# Hey Kids! Let's Visit Washington DC
## A Kids Travel Journal

Teresa Mills

Life Experiences Publishing
Bluff City, TN

This is the complementary travel journal
with activity and coloring pages to

# Hey Kids! Let's Visit WASHINGTON DC

Hey Kids! Let's Visit Washington DC
https://kid-friendly-family-vacations.com/letsvisitwdc

When you take your family trip to Washington DC, I have a free gift for you!

http://kid-friendly-family-vacations.com/wdcjournal

Copyright © 2020 by Teresa Mills

All rights reserved. No part of this publication may be reproduced, distributed or transmitted in any form or by any means, without prior written permission.

Teresa Mills/Life Experiences Publishing
PO Box 53
Bluff City, TN 37618
kid-friendly-family-vacations.com

Hey Kids! Let's Journal Washington DC/ Teresa Mills.-- 1st ed.
ISBN: 978-1-946049-08-7

# Ways To Use This Journal

This Travel Journal can be used to commemorate your visit to Washington DC in a lot of different ways.

When I was growing up, I loved keeping daily notes about all my vacations. I would make my own journal in scrap books that I purchased at a local store. With this journal in book form you do not have to cut and paste but can still be just as creative!

Have fun with writing in this journal as you travel to Washington DC!

Collect things along the way that will remind you of your trip later like receipts, ticket stubs, metro cards, flyers from hotels and attractions I visited or wanted to visit, maps, stamps, money, candy and snack wrappers... just to name a few. Attach all these things in the pages of this journal to remind you of your trip. In addition, I used to place fun items in a simple envelope and attach in my scrap book:.

Have fun with the journal and make it your own!

# My Trip to WASHINGTON DC

Draw and color a picture describing what you want to see, what you saw, or attach a photo here.

# My Trip to WASHINGTON DC

I visited Washington DC from (dates):

Thursday 5/26/22

to

Tuesday 5/31/22

I traveled to Washington DC by (how did you get there?):

plain.

The trip took (how long?)

one hour thirty minutes

Below circle how you traveled to Washington DC, or draw a picture showing how you got there!

# My Trip to WASHINGTON DC

I traveled with:

My mom, brother charlie and me

The most fun part about getting there:

I love when your ears pop and that's what happened to me.

Write more or draw a picture below about the most fun part of traveling to Washington DC.

# Favorite Food in WASHINGTON DC

Some of my most favorite foods in Washington DC: is
I like the pizza because there's a lot of cheese and I like that

Draw a picture or paste a photograph below of some of the food you tried in Washington DC.

# Favorite things
# WASHINGTON DC

My favorite thing to do in Washington DC: is going the pool because it's entertaining and I like to go under water and see everyone.

Draw a picture or paste a photograph below of your favorite thing to do Washington DC.

# Things I learned in WASHINGTON DC

Something new I learned in Washington DC:
That the Lincon memorial is facing the US capital and the Jefferson memorial is facing the white house.

Draw a picture or paste a photograph below of something new you learned in Washington DC.

*[Child's drawing in purple showing the Lincoln memorial, White house, US capitol, and Jefferson memorial, each labeled.]*

# Cool things from WASHINGTON DC

Attach some of the cool things you found and saved from Washington DC here.

# Cool things from WASHINGTON DC

Attach some of the cool things you found and saved from Washington DC here.

# Cool things from WASHINGTON DC

Attach some of the cool things you found and saved from Washington DC here.

# Cool things from WASHINGTON DC

Attach some of the cool things you found and saved from Washington DC here.

# Daily Journal
# WASHINGTON DC

Day #_____     Date: _____

Rate your day!
☆☆☆☆☆

Places visited:
_____
_____
_____
_____

My favorite part of the day:
_____
_____
_____
_____

Something special about today:
_____
_____
_____

# Daily Journal
# WASHINGTON DC

Day #_____      Date: _____

**Rate your day!**
☆☆☆☆☆

Places visited:
_____
_____
_____
_____

My favorite part of the day:
_____
_____
_____
_____

Something special about today:
_____
_____
_____
_____

# Daily Journal
# WASHINGTON DC

Day #_____       Date: _____

Rate your day!
☆☆☆☆☆

Places visited:
_____
_____
_____
_____

My favorite part of the day:
_____
_____
_____
_____

Something special about today:
_____
_____
_____

# Daily Journal
# WASHINGTON DC

Day #_____          Date: _____

Rate your day!
☆☆☆☆☆

Places visited:
_____
_____
_____
_____

My favorite part of the day:
_____
_____
_____
_____

Something special about today:
_____
_____
_____

# Daily Journal
# WASHINGTON DC

Day #_____        Date: _____

Rate your day!
☆☆☆☆☆

Places visited:
_____
_____
_____
_____

My favorite part of the day:
_____
_____
_____
_____

Something special about today:
_____
_____
_____

# Daily Journal
# WASHINGTON DC

Day #_____          Date: _____

Rate your day!
☆ ☆ ☆ ☆ ☆

Places visited:
_____
_____
_____
_____

My favorite part of the day:
_____
_____
_____
_____

Something special about today:
_____
_____
_____

# Daily Journal
# WASHINGTON DC

Day #_____     Date: _____

Rate your day!
☆☆☆☆☆

Places visited:
_____
_____
_____
_____

My favorite part of the day:
_____
_____
_____
_____

Something special about today:
_____
_____
_____

# Daily Journal
# WASHINGTON DC

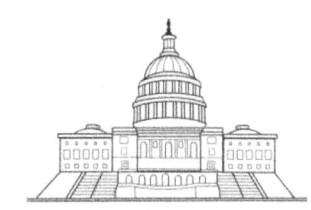

Day #_____      Date: _____

Rate your day!
☆☆☆☆☆

Places visited:
_____
_____
_____
_____

My favorite part of the day:
_____
_____
_____
_____

Something special about today:
_____
_____
_____

# Daily Journal
# WASHINGTON DC

Day #_____     Date: _____

Rate your day!
☆☆☆☆☆

Places visited:
_____
_____
_____
_____
_____

My favorite part of the day:
_____
_____
_____
_____

Something special about today:
_____
_____
_____

# Daily Journal
# WASHINGTON DC

Day #_____      Date: _____

Rate your day!
☆ ☆ ☆ ☆ ☆

Places visited:
_____
_____
_____
_____

My favorite part of the day:
_____
_____
_____
_____

Something special about today:
_____
_____
_____

# ACTIVITY AND COLORING PAGES

# THE WHITE HOUSE

Find these white house related words in the grid below. The words can be in the grid vertical, horizontal, or diagonal and either forward or backward.

```
T W N K L W G N V L V N R Y P R
Q N W A S H I N G T O N D C E E
E G E Q E N O E N I R A M M N X
N E N D T V W N V K B Q O N N E
O C K Y I L G L M R G O H W S C
E N Q P T S D P E F R Y E K Y U
C E E B H L E K I N K S W T L T
R D B A T N N R O W T B Q W V I
O I L C S U S I P W D L W K A V
F S M Q B T T N I L W N B N N E
R E R F L A W N P M Z F M N I J
I R V A U F G I T T F W Z D A C
A C D T C A B I N E T B K Y A Z
W Y I W C H F T Q G Y Z M K V Q
D S P L X W H I T E H O U S E Q
L L I B R A L L O D Y T N E W T
```

air force one
bunker
cabinet
east wing
executive
first lady
marine one
pennsylvania ave
president
residence
situation room
twenty dollar bill
washington dc
west wing
white house

# CAPITOL DOME GRID

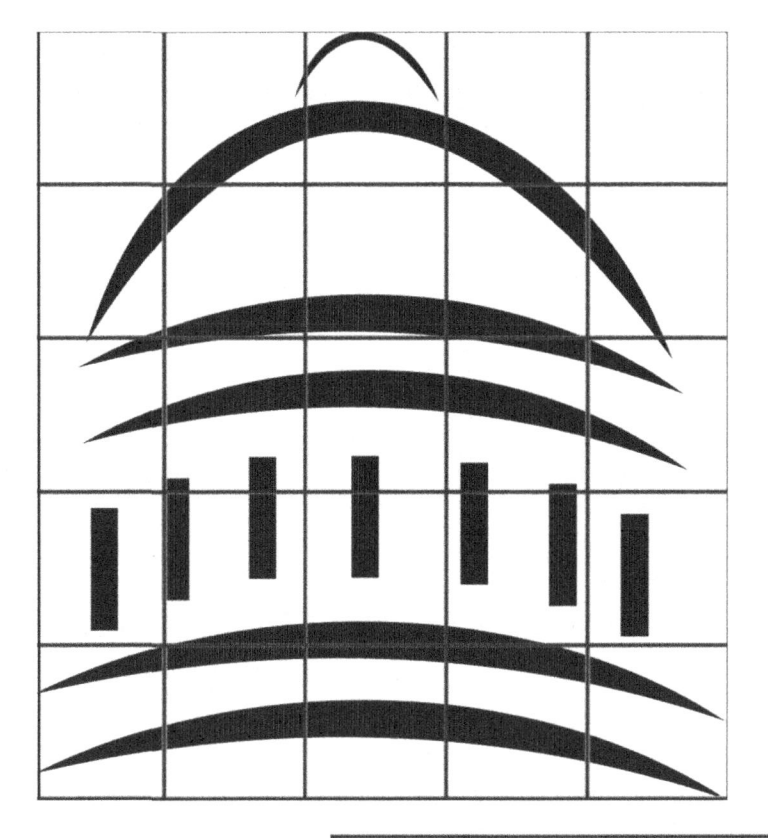

Can you draw the US Capitol dome in the grid below from the drawing on the left?

Just draw each block in the grid one by one and before you know it, you will have drawn the US Capitol dome!

One block is filled in for you as a starting point.

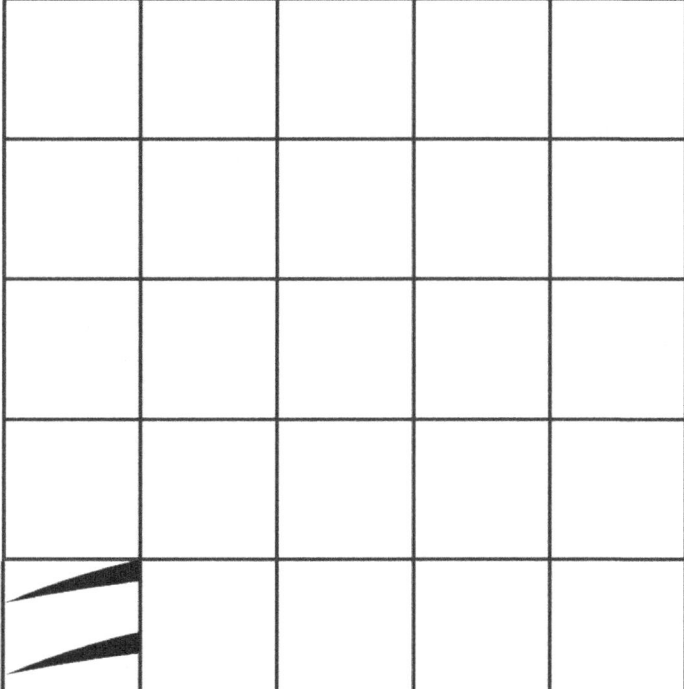

# NATIONAL CATHEDRAL

Strolling through the National Cathedral gardens is like winding through a maze  Start at "ENTER" and wind your way through the maze "EXIT".  Beware, there may be cross-overs in the path of the maze (a cross-over is when the path of the maze crosses over the top of another portion of the maze – sort of like a bridge.)

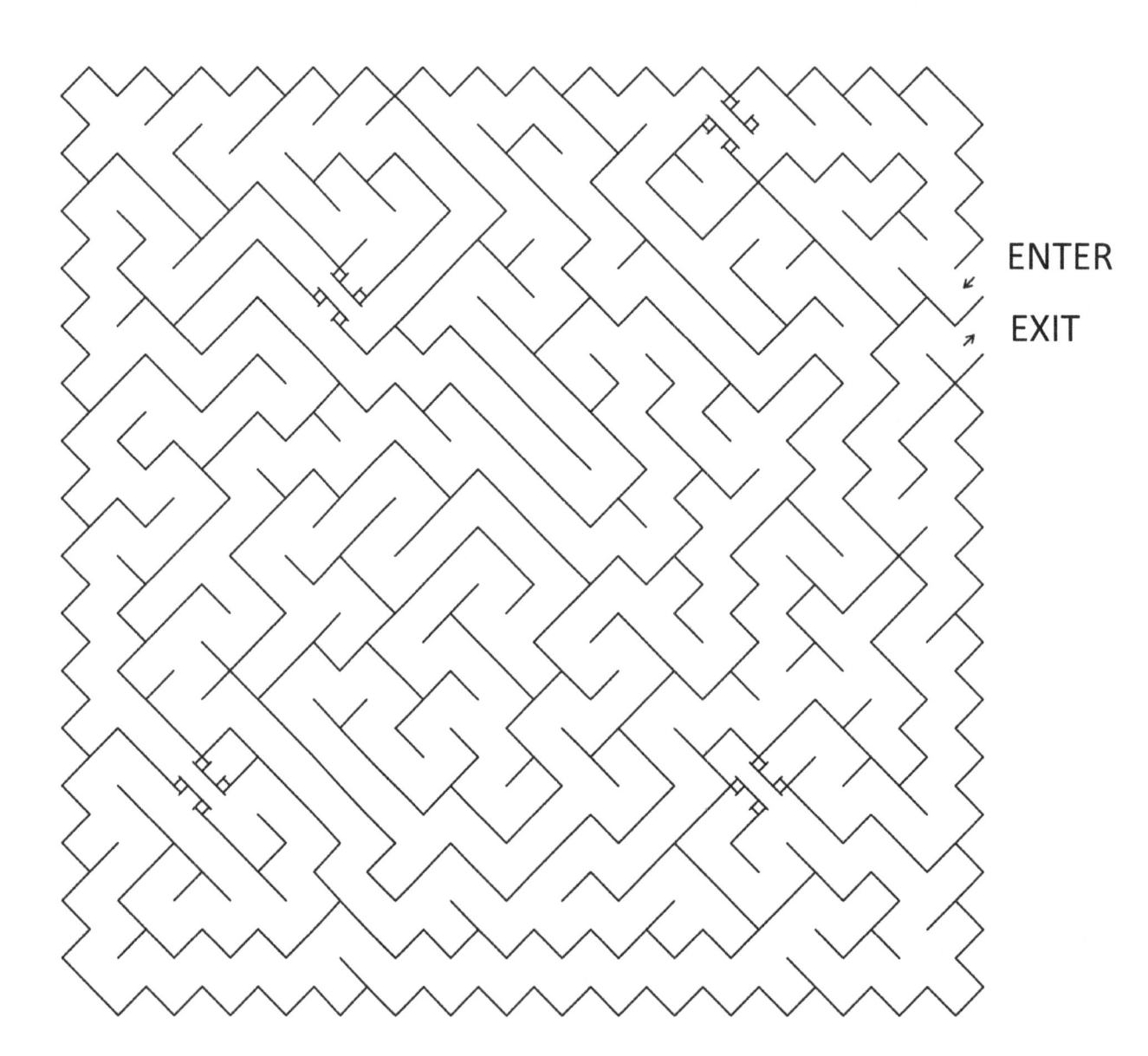

ENTER

EXIT

# WDC ANAGRAMS

Unscramble the words in the puzzle to reveal a Washington DC related word. The lines for each anagram tell you have many new words you will make. Don't forget to check the Word Bank below for more hints.

1. ewe shout hi  _____  _____

2. no men must  _____

3. swing no hat  _____

4. a zit on a loon  _____  _____

5. not in the snowman mug  _____  _____

6. cornmeal million  _____  _____

7. ma and i measure cups  _____  _____
   _____  _____

8. no tall animal  _____  _____

9. soft red heart  _____  _____

10. i lost a cup  _____  _____

---

**WORD BANK**
US Capitol    Lincoln Memorial    Air and space museum    National Mall
Fords Theater    White House    Monuments    Washington    National Zoo
Washington Monument

# REFLECTING POOL LETTERDROP

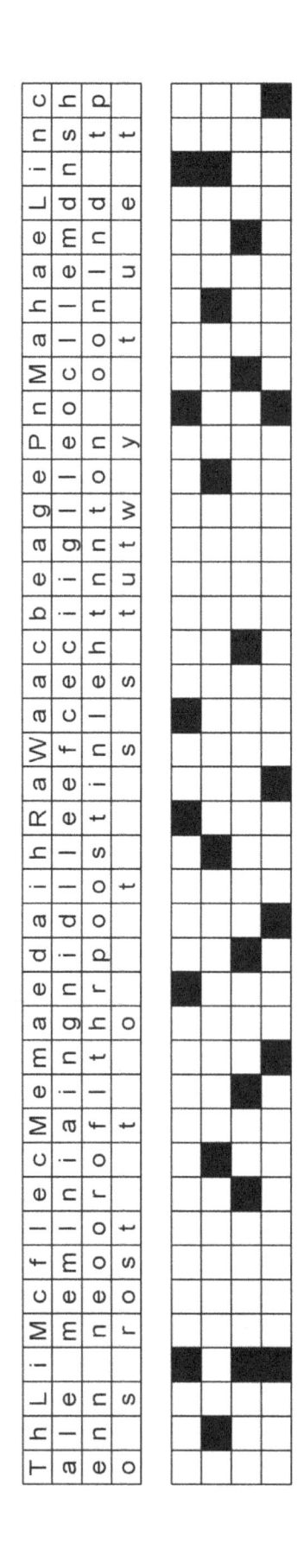

| T | h | L | i | M | c | f | l | e | c | M | e | m | a | e | d | a | i | h | R | a | W | a | a | c | b | e | a | g | e | P | n | M | a | h | a | e | L | i | n | c |
| a | l | e | | | | m | e | m | i | n | i | a | i | n | g | n | i | d | l | e | e | f | c | e | c | i | g | i | l | e | o | c | l | i | e | m | d | n | s | h |
| e | n | n | | | | n | e | o | o | r | o | f | l | t | h | r | p | o | o | s | t | i | n | l | e | h | t | n | n | t | o | o | n | l | n | d | | t | p | |
| o | s | | | | | r | o | s | t | | | | | | | t | | | | | | | | | | | | | t | u | | t | w | y | t | u | e | | | |

This letterdrop puzzle contains a quote about the Lincoln Memorial Reflecting Pool. Use the letters in each column to fill in the boxes below them to form words. The letters may or may not go into the boxes in the same order that they appear. Once a letter is used, cross it off as it will not be used again. A dark square represents the end of a word.

# JEFFERSON MEMORIAL

Can you help Susie get to the Jefferson Memorial?

# CONNECT THE DOTS PLUS+

Connect all the dots in order, starting at 1 to complete the picture, but this picture has some parts missing once you connect the dots. So, after you connect all the dots, complete and color this picture.

# WDC CROSSWORD

## WORD BANK
Abraham Lincoln
Bureau of Engraving and Printing
Capitol
Congress
Fords Theater
George Washington
Inauguration
Jefferson Memorial
Lincoln Memorial
memorials
metro
monuments
museums
National Cathedral
National Cemetery
National Mall
National Zoo
obelisk
Thomas Jefferson
Washington Monument
White House

## ACROSS

1 monument with a bronze statue of the third president
4 where US currency is printed
7 where congress meets
8 governing body of the USA
9 third president of the USA
10 it's not a shopping center
11 the shape of the Washington Monument
12 an historical place to see a play
13 a way to get around Washington DC
15 world's largest obelisk
17 formal admission to office
18 US military place of final rest
19 National house of prayer
20 1600 Pennsylvania Ave
21 a structure to commemorate someone

## DOWN

2 memorial to Abraham Lincoln
3 places to view pieces of history
5 president shot at Ford's Theater
6 first president of the USA
14 home to pandas and gorillas
16 structures of historical importance

# WORD COUNT

How many different words can you make from Washington DC?

## WASHINGTON DC

_____   _____   _____

_____   _____   _____

_____   _____   _____

_____   _____   _____

_____   _____   _____

_____   _____   _____

_____   _____   _____

_____   _____   _____

_____   _____   _____

_____   _____   _____

# COIN MATCH GAME

Can you match the front of the coin on the left with the back of the coin on the right? The names of the president on each coin is listed on the left.

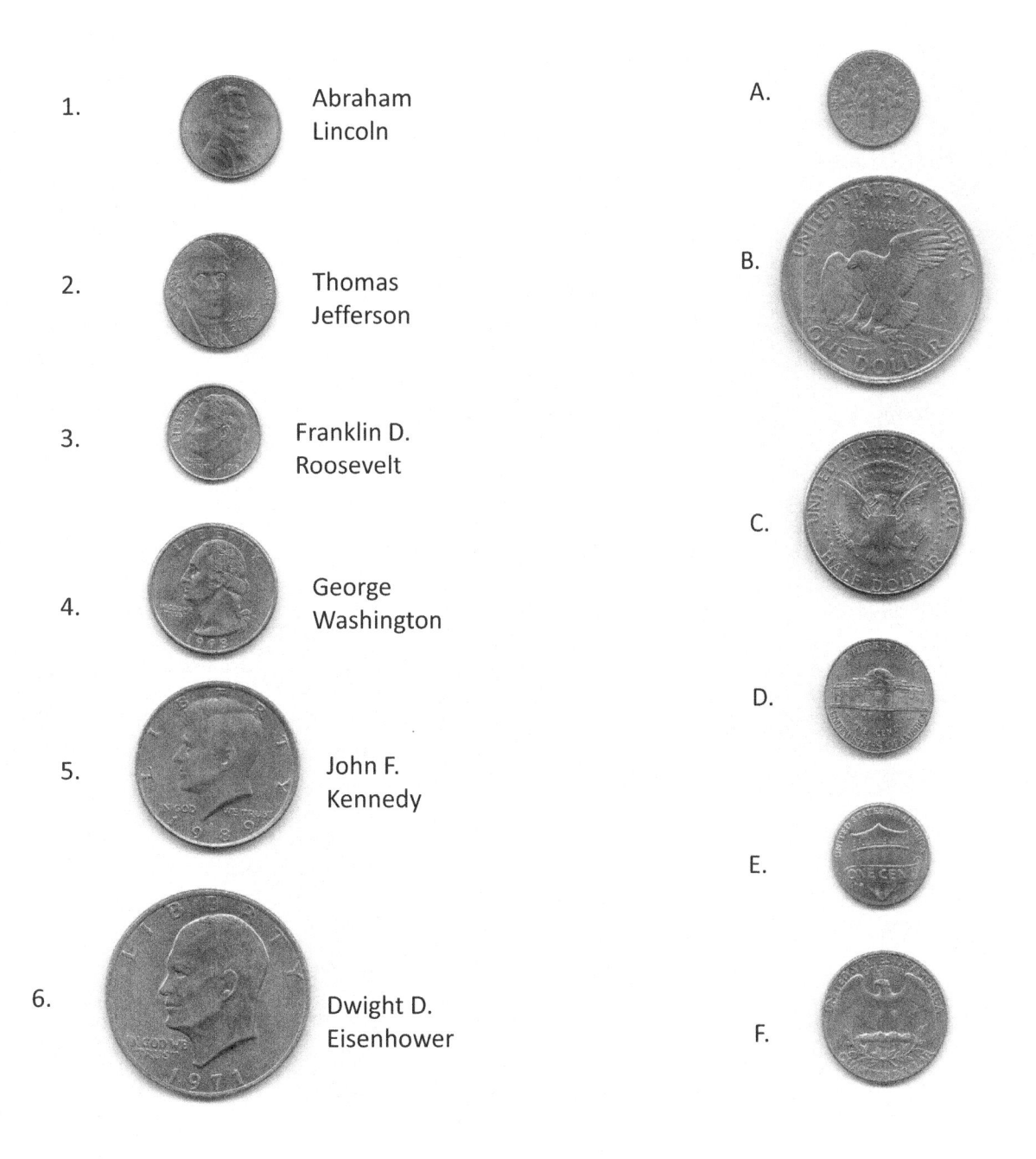

1. Abraham Lincoln

2. Thomas Jefferson

3. Franklin D. Roosevelt

4. George Washington

5. John F. Kennedy

6. Dwight D. Eisenhower

A.

B.

C.

D.

E.

F.

# BILL MATCH GAME

Can you place the correct face on each bill?

1.  Alexander Hamilton
2.  Thomas Jefferson
3.  Ulysses Grant
4.  George Washington
5.  Andrew Jackson
6.  Benjamin Franklin
7.  Abraham Lincoln

A. $1 bill
B. $2 bill
C. $5 bill
D. $10 bill
E. $20 bill
F. $50 bill
G. $100 bill

# DECODE THE MESSAGE

Can you decode this message about Ford's Theater? Each number below the space matches a number in the key found above the puzzle. Place the correct letter in each space by using the key. to complete a phrase.

| 1 | 2 | 3 | 4 | 5 | 6 | 7 | 8 | 9 | 10 | 11 | 12 | 13 |
|---|---|---|---|---|---|---|---|---|----|----|----|----|
| Z | F | M | P | Q | O | W | V | L | T  | E  | G  | X  |

| 14 | 15 | 16 | 17 | 18 | 19 | 20 | 21 | 22 | 23 | 24 | 25 | 26 |
|----|----|----|----|----|----|----|----|----|----|----|----|----|
| I  | K  | H  | Y  | J  | C  | B  | A  | D  | S  | R  | U  | N  |

___ ___ ___ ___ ___ ___ ___ ___ ___   ___ ___ ___ ___ ___ ___ ___
 4  24  11  23  14  22  11  26  10   21  20  24  21  16  21   3

___ ___ ___ ___ ___ ___ ___   ___ ___ ___
 9  14  26  19   6   9  26    7  21  23

___ ___ ___ ___ ___ ___ ___ ___ ___ ___ ___ ___   ___ ___
21  23  23  21  23  23  14  26  21  10  11  22   21  10

___ ___ ___ ___ ___   ___ ___ ___ ___ ___ ___ ___
 2   6  24  22  23   10  16  11  21  10  11  24

In the space below, can you write a code message about your favorite place to visit in Washington DC?

# ZOO CONNECT THE DOTS

Connect all the dots in order, starting at 1 to complete the picture. After you connect all the dots, you can color the picture and draw a scene around it.

# ZOO WORD FIND

```
B D K N N A K T E F D X R R B M I G U A N A Z Z
K L M L X B L S R H Q A O Q M E K R P R T Q C C
R T K Z H F R L C R C P T P R B A G K Q F M N V
R N N L R O N Y I A M W A F T A K R E E M K V J
G B N O H M E K P R L Q G P E Q Y T A C B O B C
N O G M L F V L U L O H I E B R T B P T A O G B
Z T D W K L A K G D K G L Y S J R Q A J N N H R
S E T E M C R G O D U P L H W I R E C L O C T G
T P B K I L U B H G C M A N S E O R T G L H D P
I B K R C R T D L T K Z N E D I O T A P A A M A
N E M N A R I B N G E R Y N S C F R R T N K W N
G A H R Q T I A P G L B A T O O D T E O P F Z D
R V Y L W S H A R L G M S D M R O E A N T F W A
A E G E O P R F T P A C I E E L H G O C E M U J
Y R N N E R L O R L E L O T A C T J N T N Q M N
C G R L O I T X A L E K A B P L N D N O T Q Z M
R L E T Z I M S Q Z P W G J R H O B N K M E F B
A T Z A G R Q N N A C I L E P A E B V E H J R Y
N T R E Y L T Q C H I N C H I L L A G L L H C E
E D R M C J V Q B A S I L I S K E R C T I Y N K
K B H T W W Y E K N O D R L Q T M R H R O H J N
G L O P O S S U M T V W O L F F A L L U N N Y O
T S E A L I O N R Q N M Y R P N H W L T N H C M
E K A N S E L T T A R D T Y Q F C G M Z G N X W
```

| | | | | |
|---|---|---|---|---|
| alligator | cobra | goat | newt | seal |
| alpaca | crane | gorilla | opossum | stingray |
| basilisk | crocodile | hog | otter | tiger |
| bear | donkey | horse | panda | tortoise |
| beaver | duck | iguana | parrot | turtle |
| bison | eagle | kudu | pelican | wallaby |
| bobcat | elephant | lion | prairie dog | water |
| catfish | emu | lizard | rattlesnake | dragon |
| chameleon | ferret | meerkat | raven | wolf |
| cheetah | fox | mongoose | salamander | zebra |
| chinchilla | frog | monkey | sea lion | |

## The White House

The White House is the home and workplace of the President of the United States of America. It is located at 1600 Pennsylvania Avenue in Washington DC.

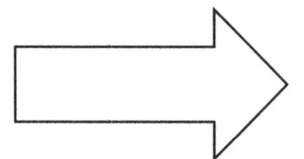

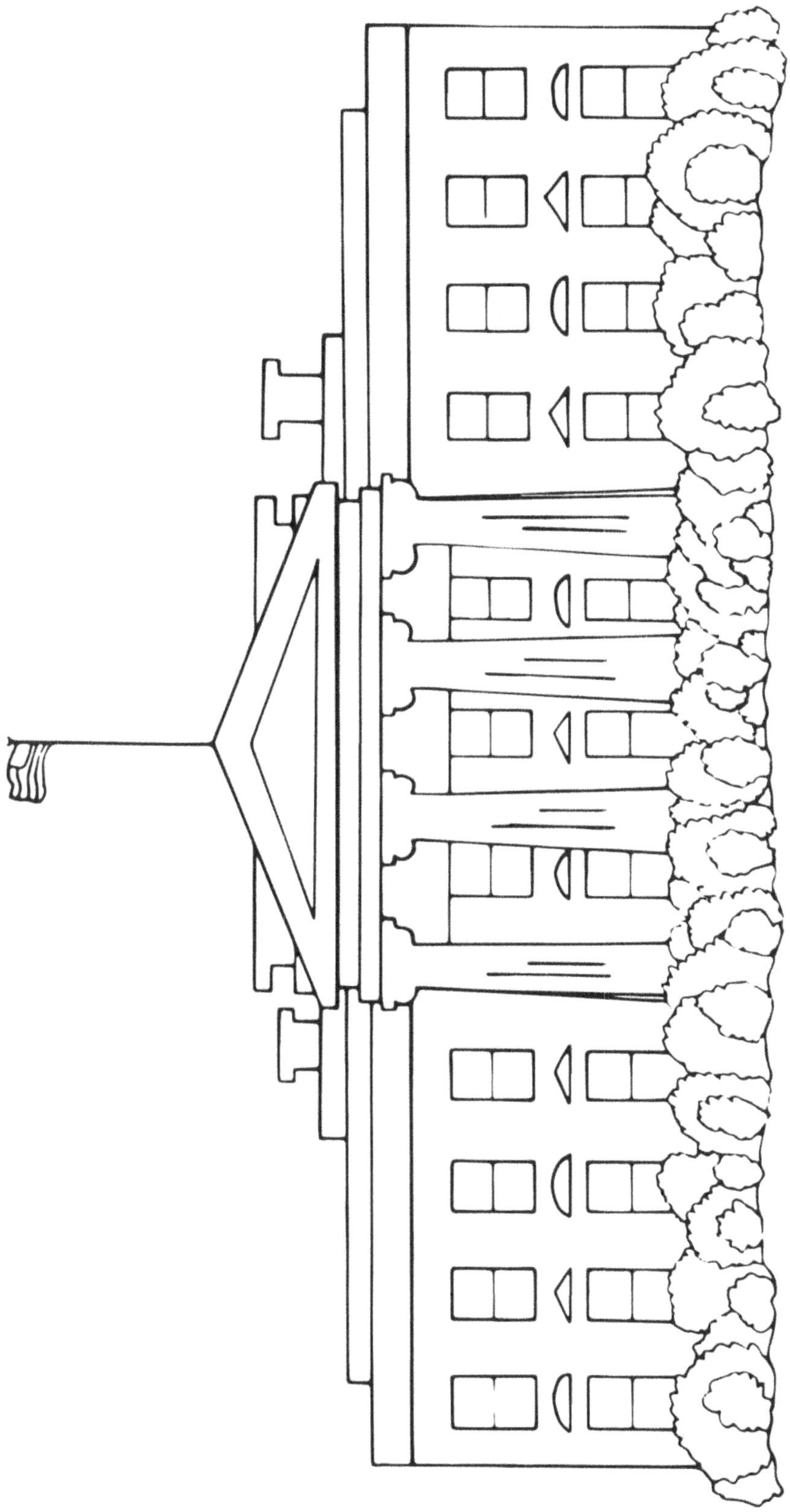

## The US Capitol

The United States Capitol Building is where the United States Congress meets. The Congress is made up of the Senate and the House of Representatives.

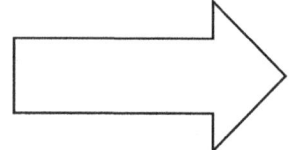

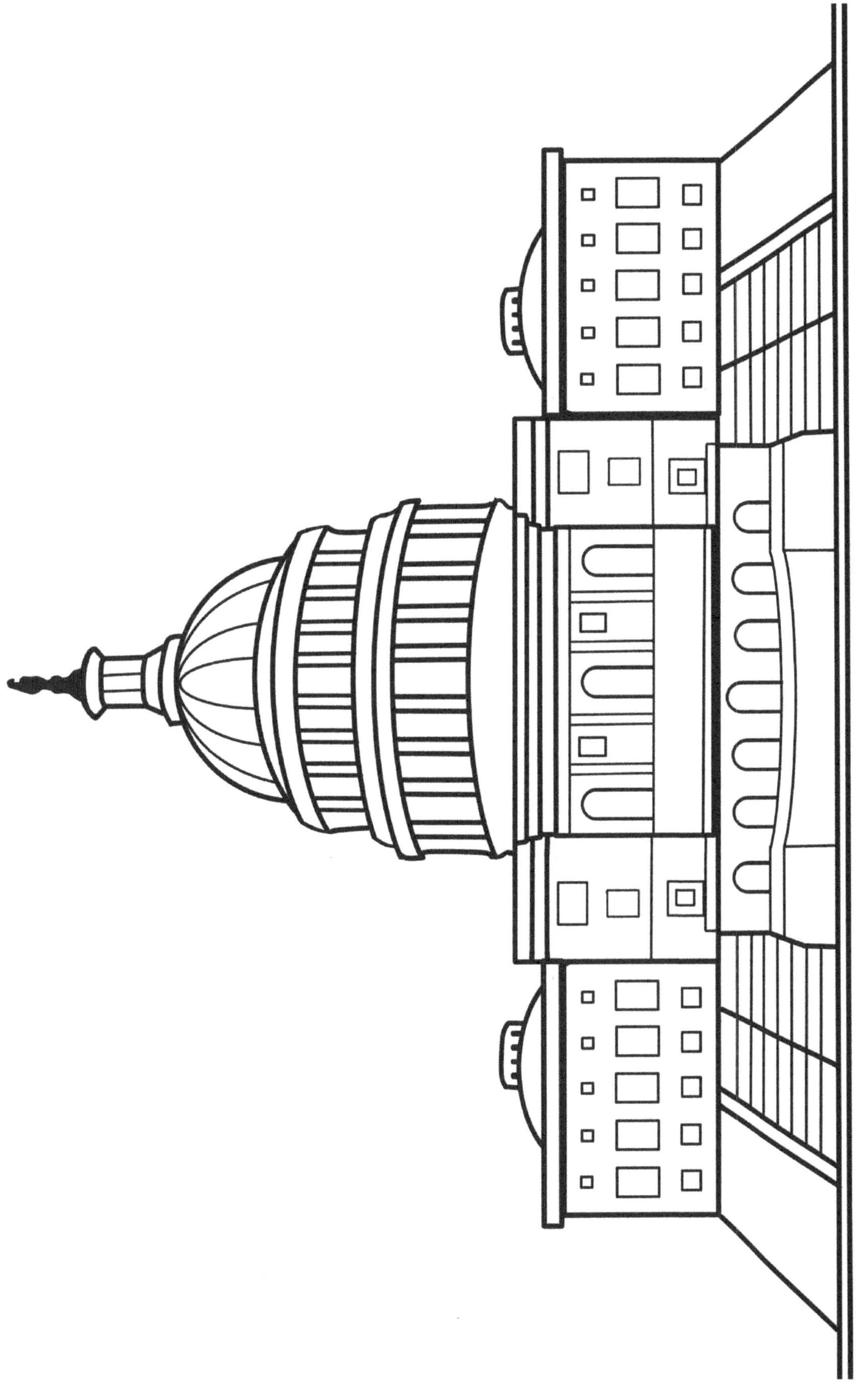

## The National Cathedral

The Washington National Cathedral is a part of the Episcopal Church. The United States Congress has named the Cathedral the "National House of Prayer".

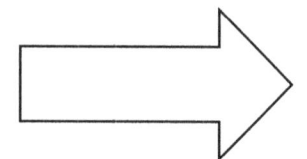

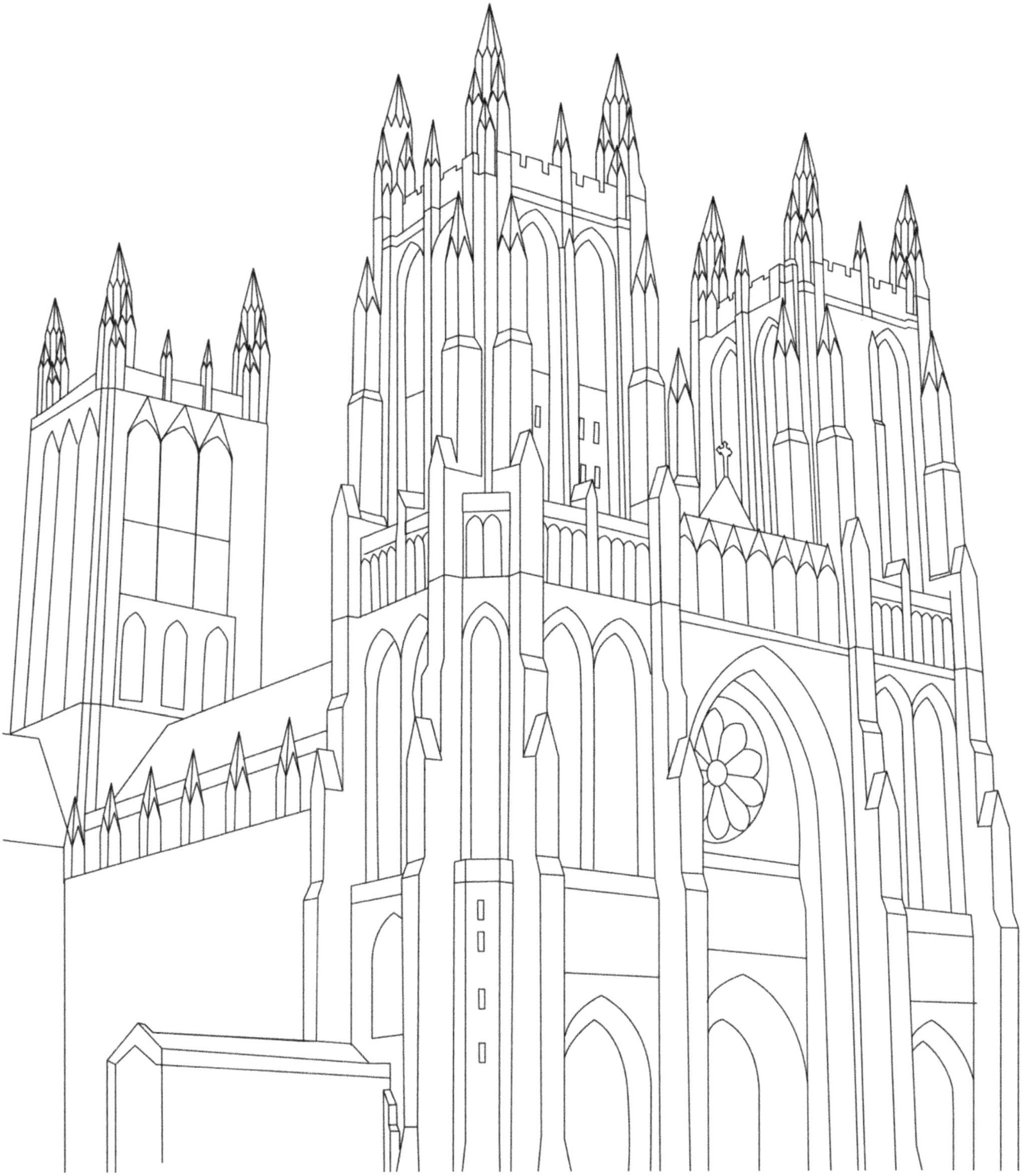

## Arlington National Cemetery

The Arlington National Cemetery is a "United States Military Cemetery". It is a 624-acre cemetery located just across the Potomac River from Washington DC in Arlington, Virginia.

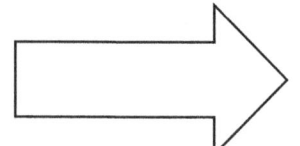

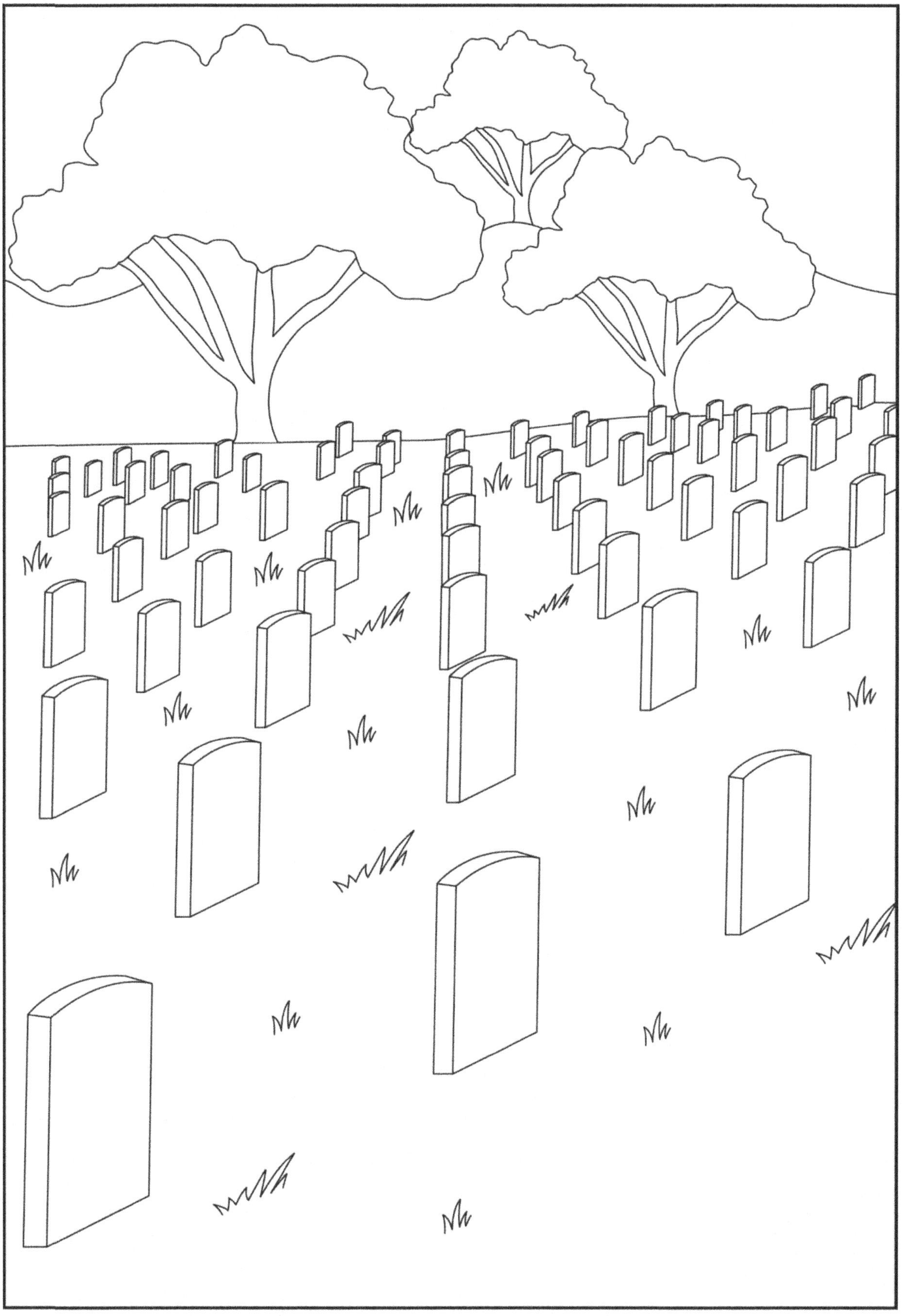

## Arlington National Cemetery

The Arlington National Cemetery is the home of the Tomb of the Unknowns. This is a memorial to all American soldiers who died in war but were unidentified.

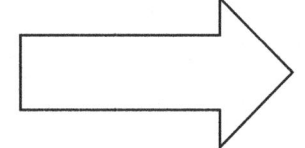

HERE RESTS IN
HONORED GLORY
AN AMERICAN
SOLDIER

KNOWN BUT TO GOD

## National Mall Reflecting Pool

The reflecting pool is called the Lincoln Memorial Reflecting Pool and spans most of the distance between the Lincoln Memorial to the Washington Monument.

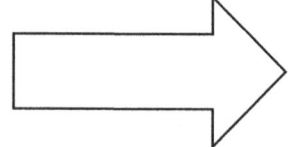

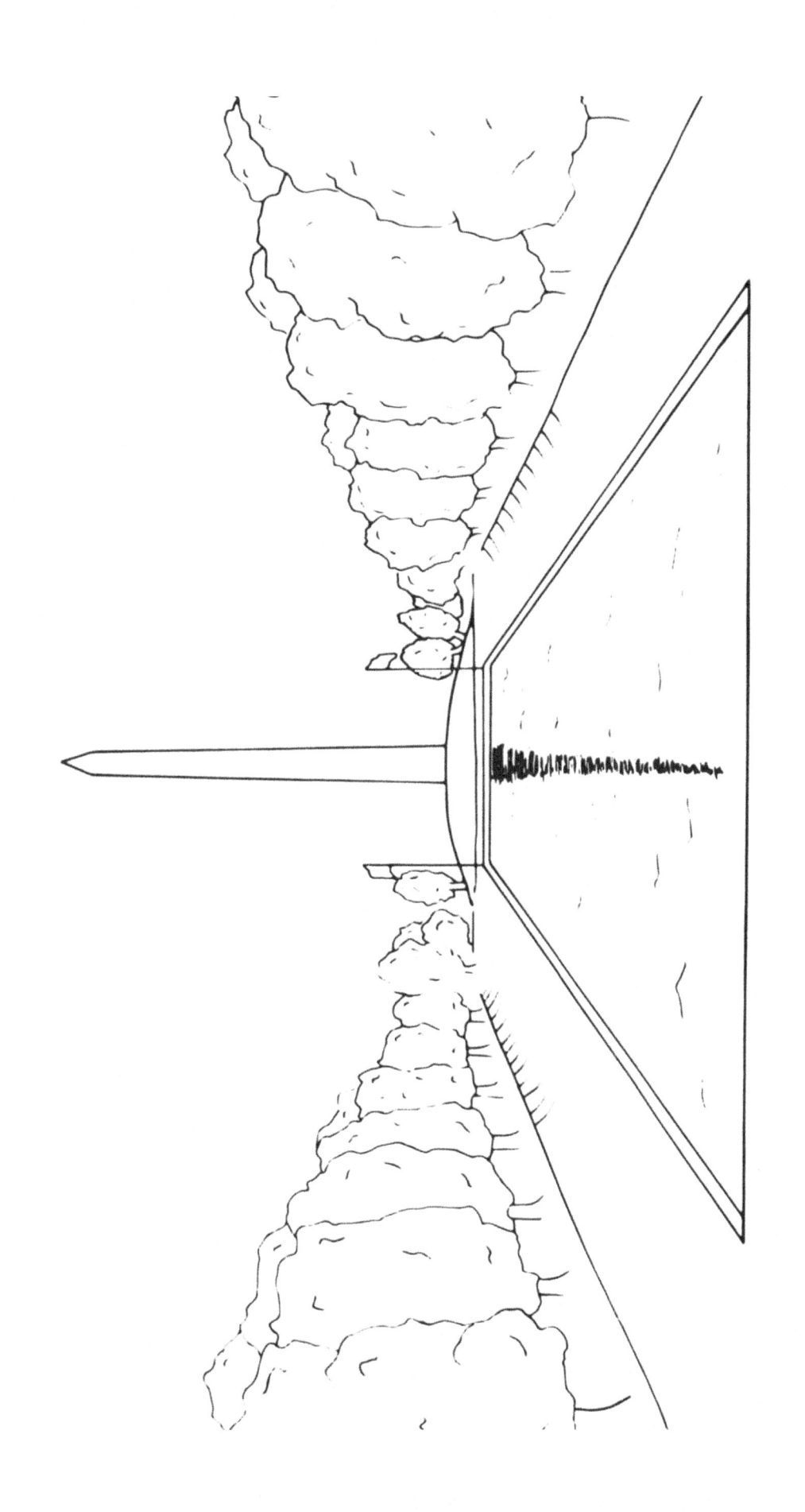

## Washington Monument

The Washington Monument stands on the National Mall in Washington DC and is a memorial for the first president of the United States, George Washington.

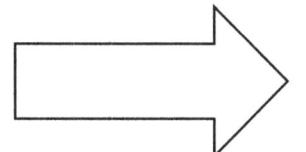

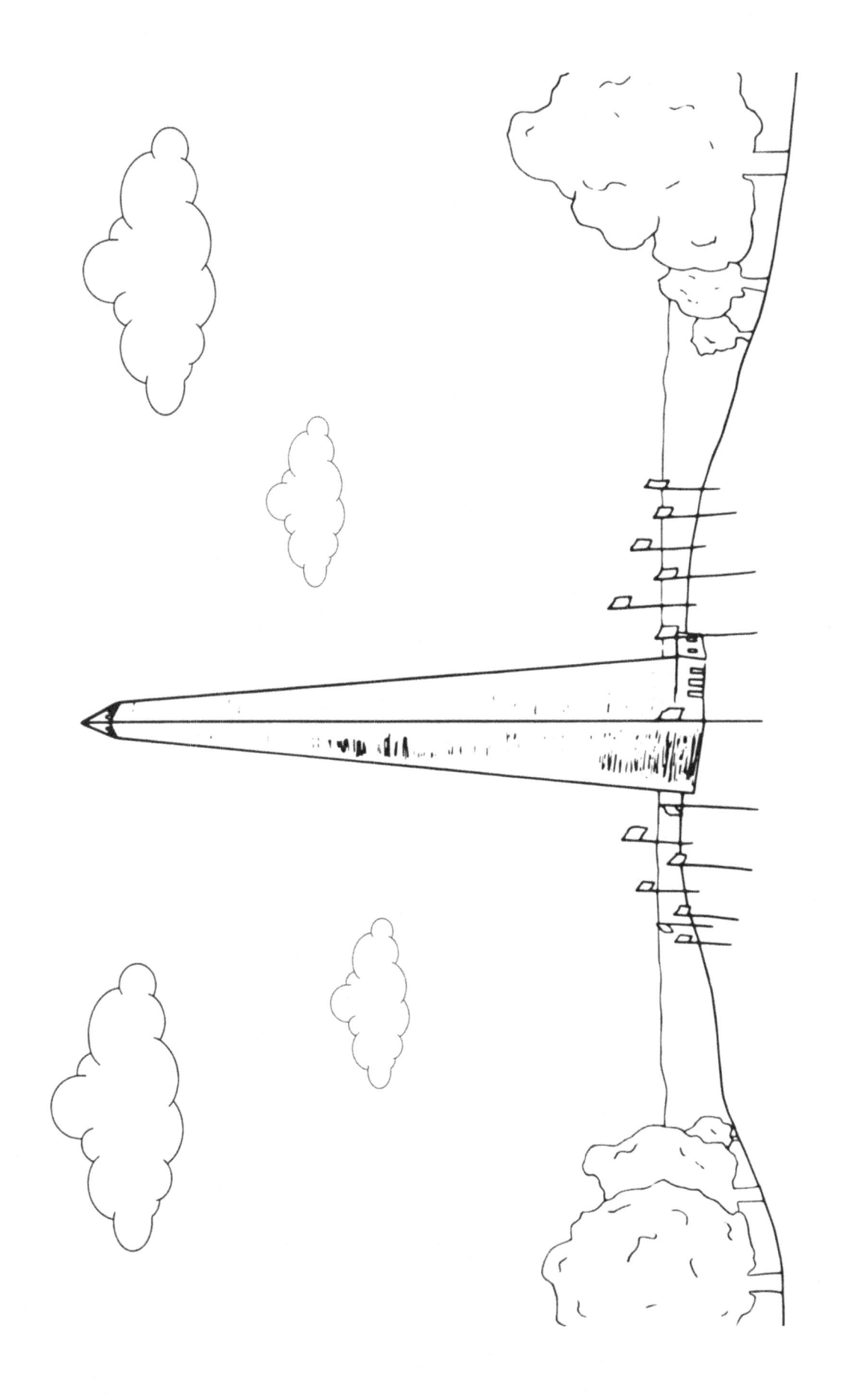

## Lincoln Memorial

The Lincoln Memorial is a memorial to Abraham Lincoln, the 16th President of the United States of America. It is located on the western end of the National Mall, across the reflecting pool from the Washington Monument.

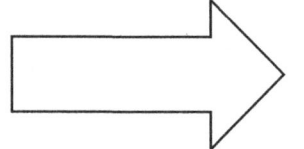

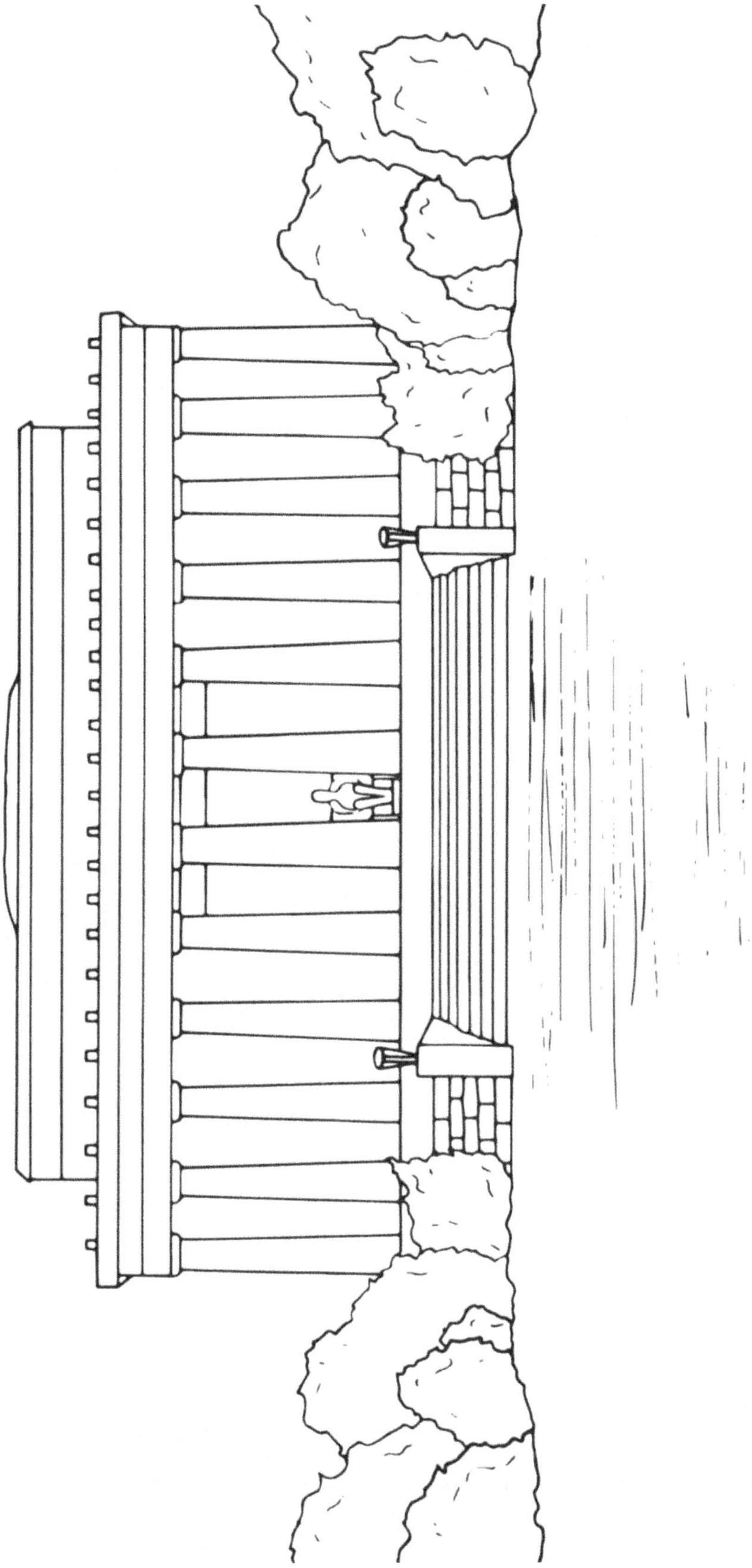

## Lincoln Memorial

The monument building is large and inside it is a large seated sculpture of Abraham Lincoln. The sculptor of the statue of Abraham Lincoln was Daniel Chester French.

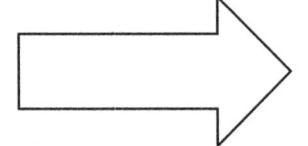

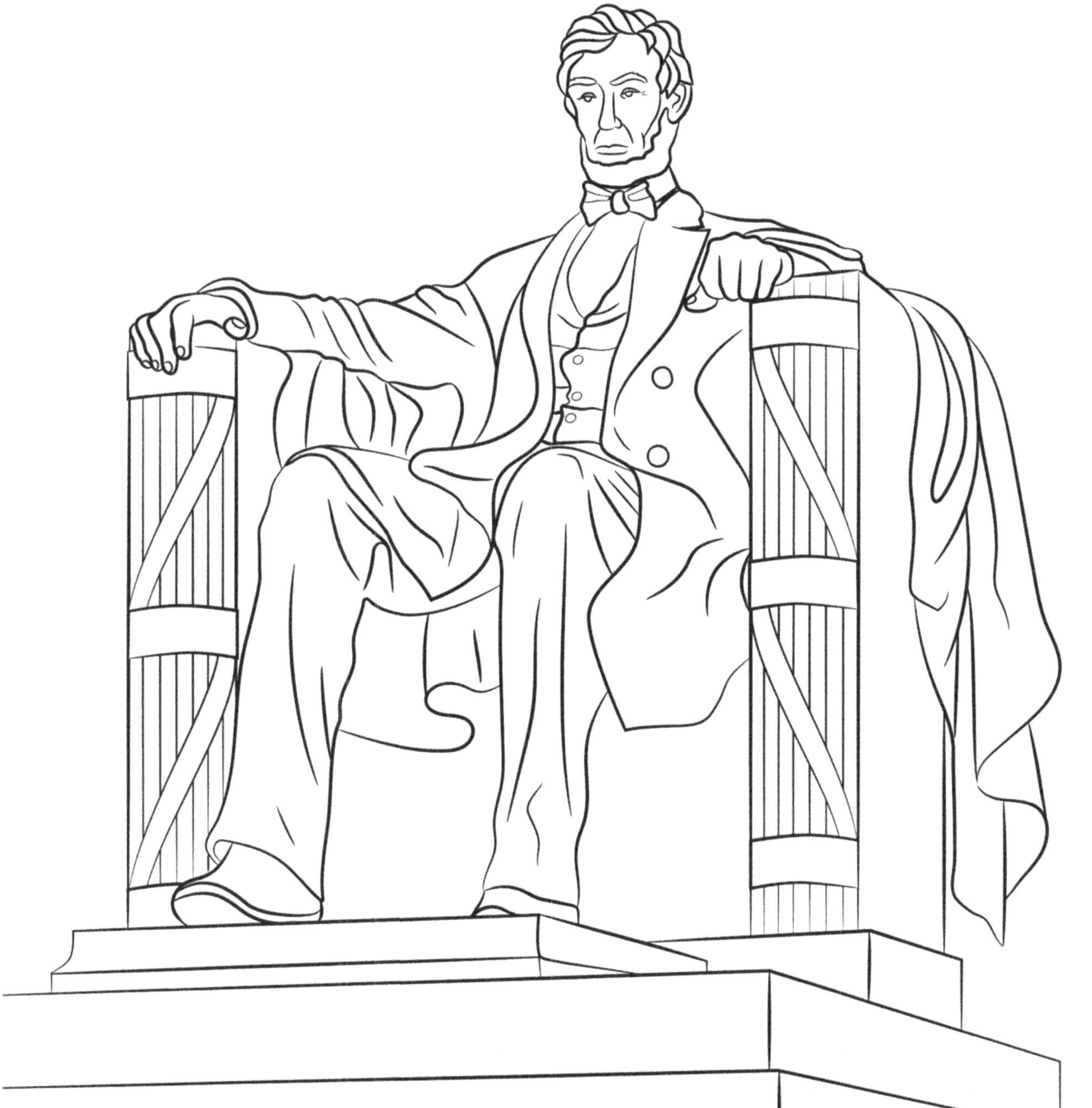

## Jefferson Memorial

The Jefferson Memorial is dedicated to Thomas Jefferson, the main drafter and writer of the "Declaration of Independence". Thomas Jefferson was the third President of the United States of America.

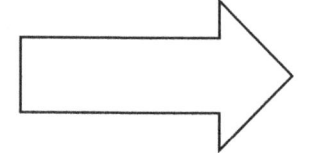

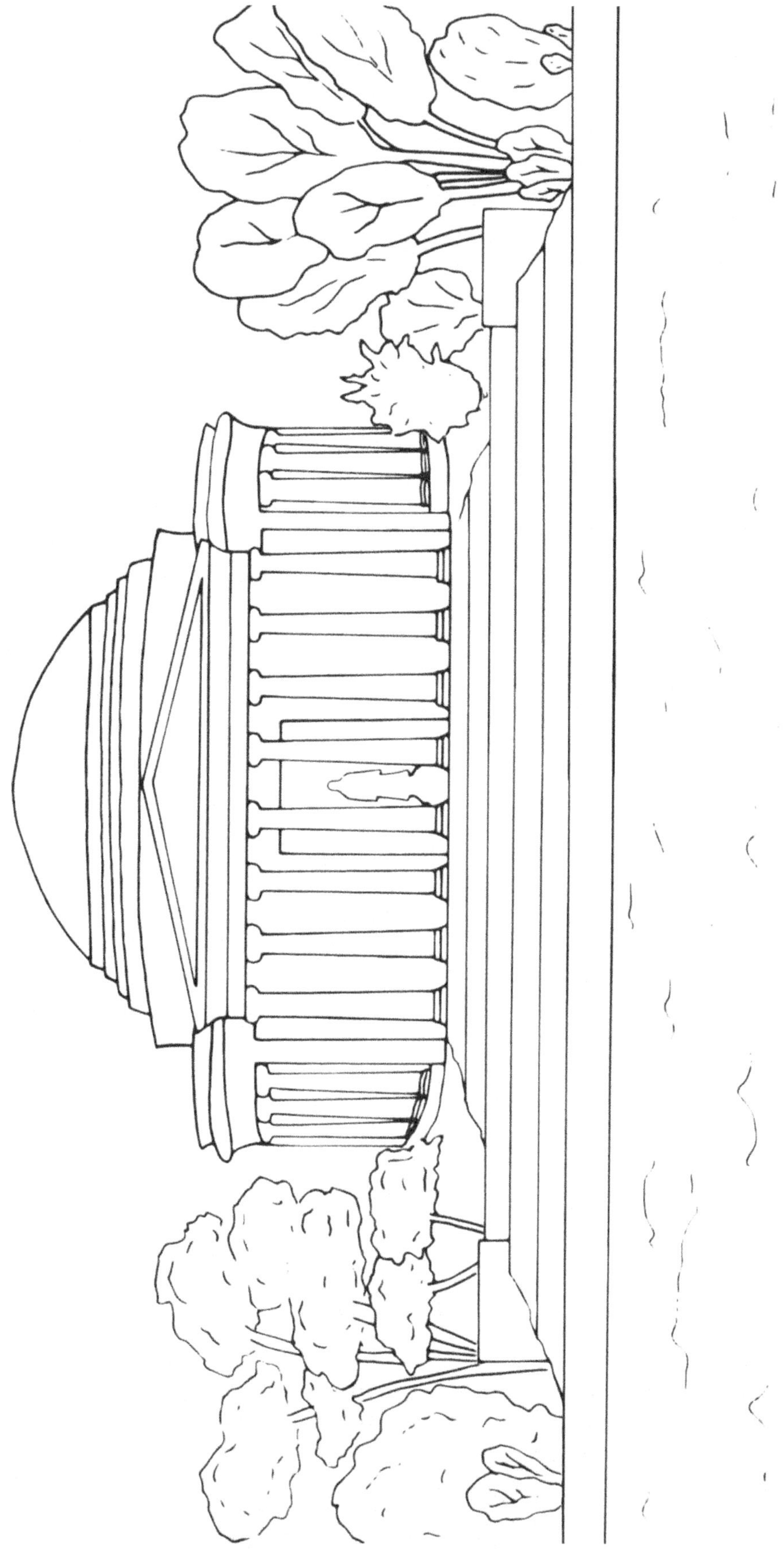

## Smithsonian Institution Building

The Smithsonian Institute has many museums located along the National Mall and around Washington DC.  This is the Smithsonian Castle 0 the home of the Smithsonian Welcome Center.

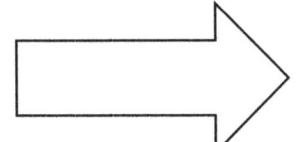

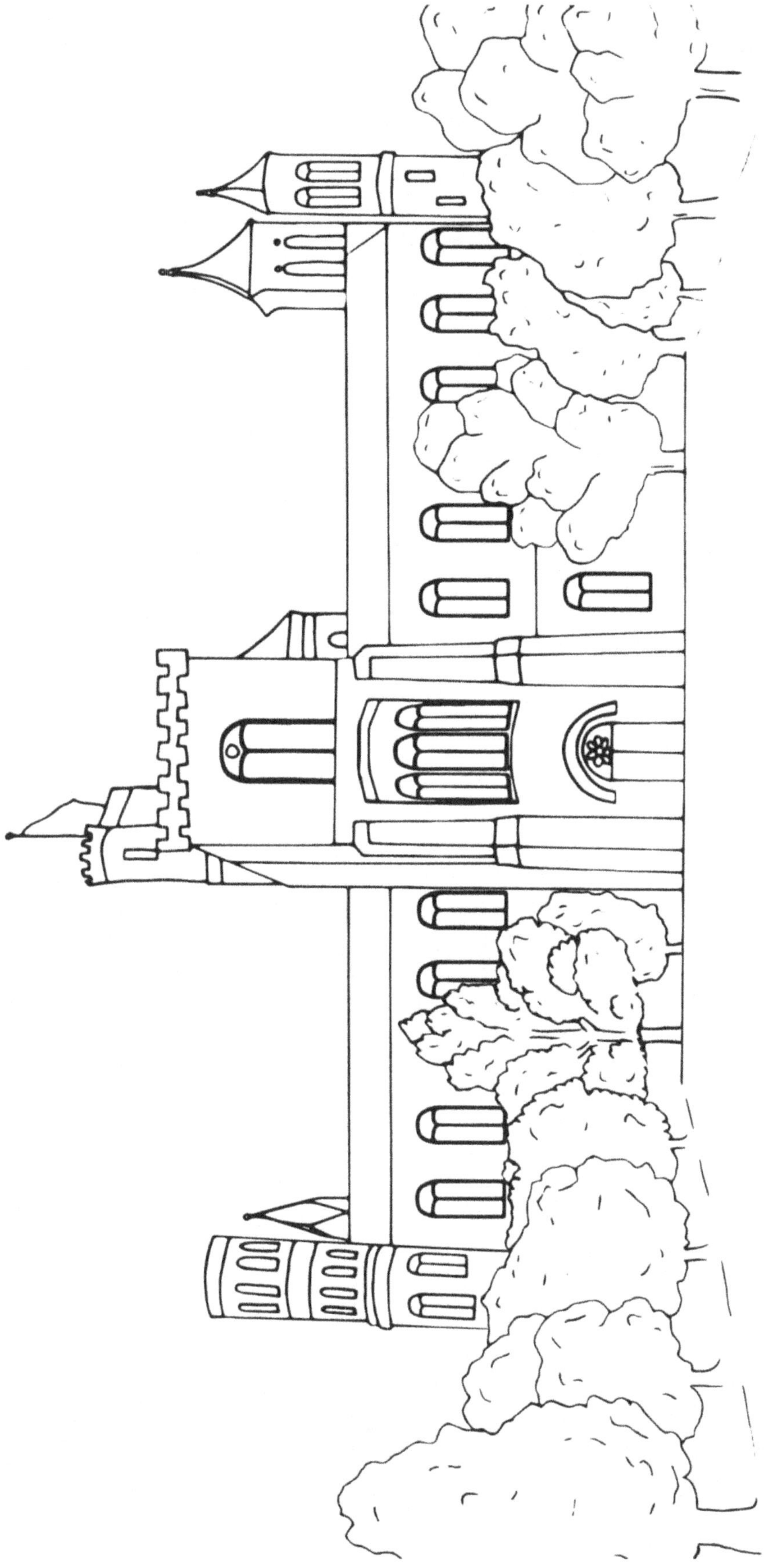

## Smithsonian Air and Space Museum

The main campus of the National Air and Space Museum is on the National Mall and is one of the museums of the Smithsonian Institution. It opened its main building to the public in 1976 and gets close to 7 million visitors a year!

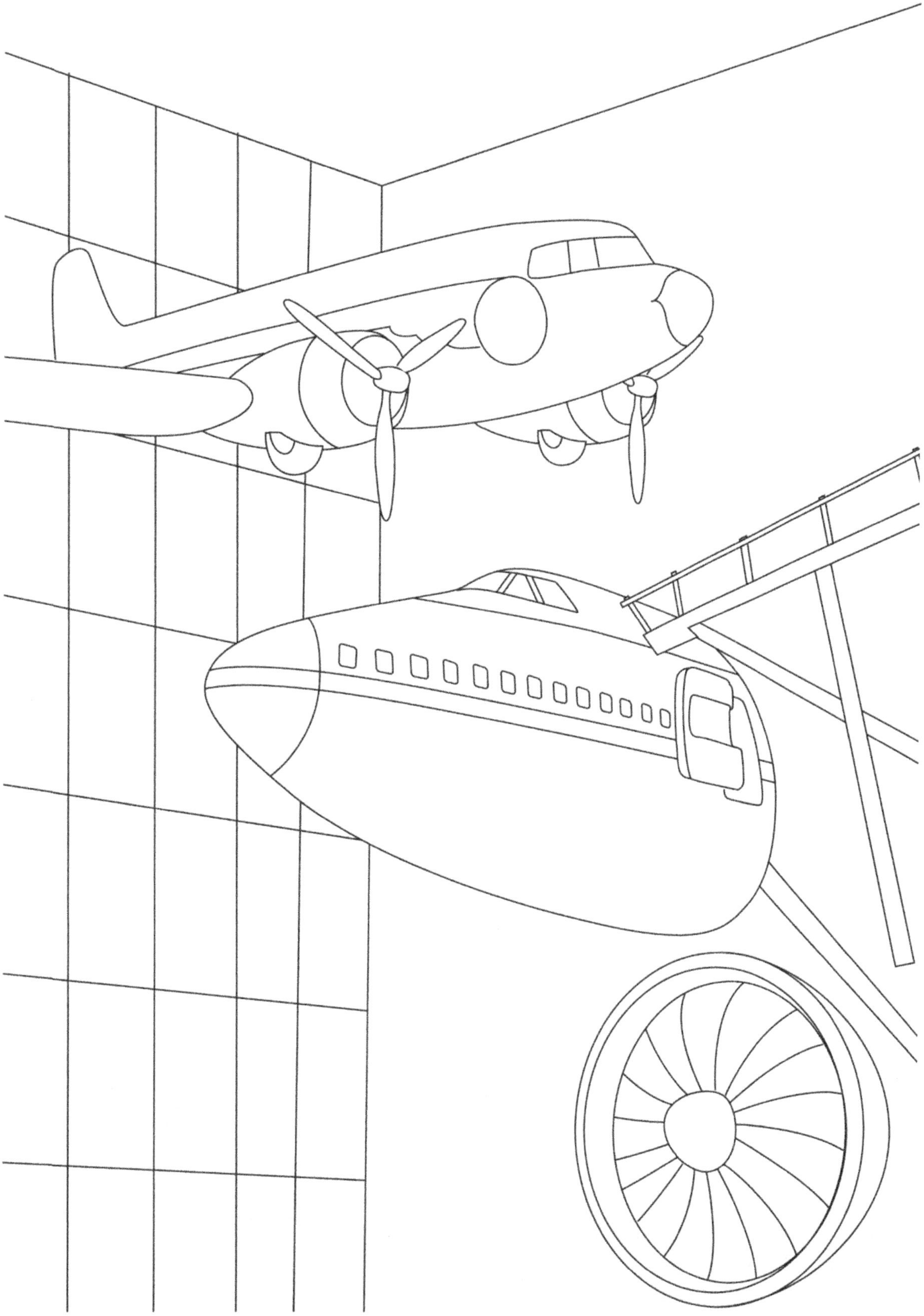

## Smithsonian Museum of Natural History

The National Museum of Natural History is part of the Smithsonian Institution and is located on the National Mall in Washington DC. This museum is dedicated to the knowledge of the natural world!

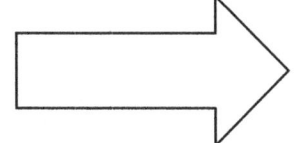

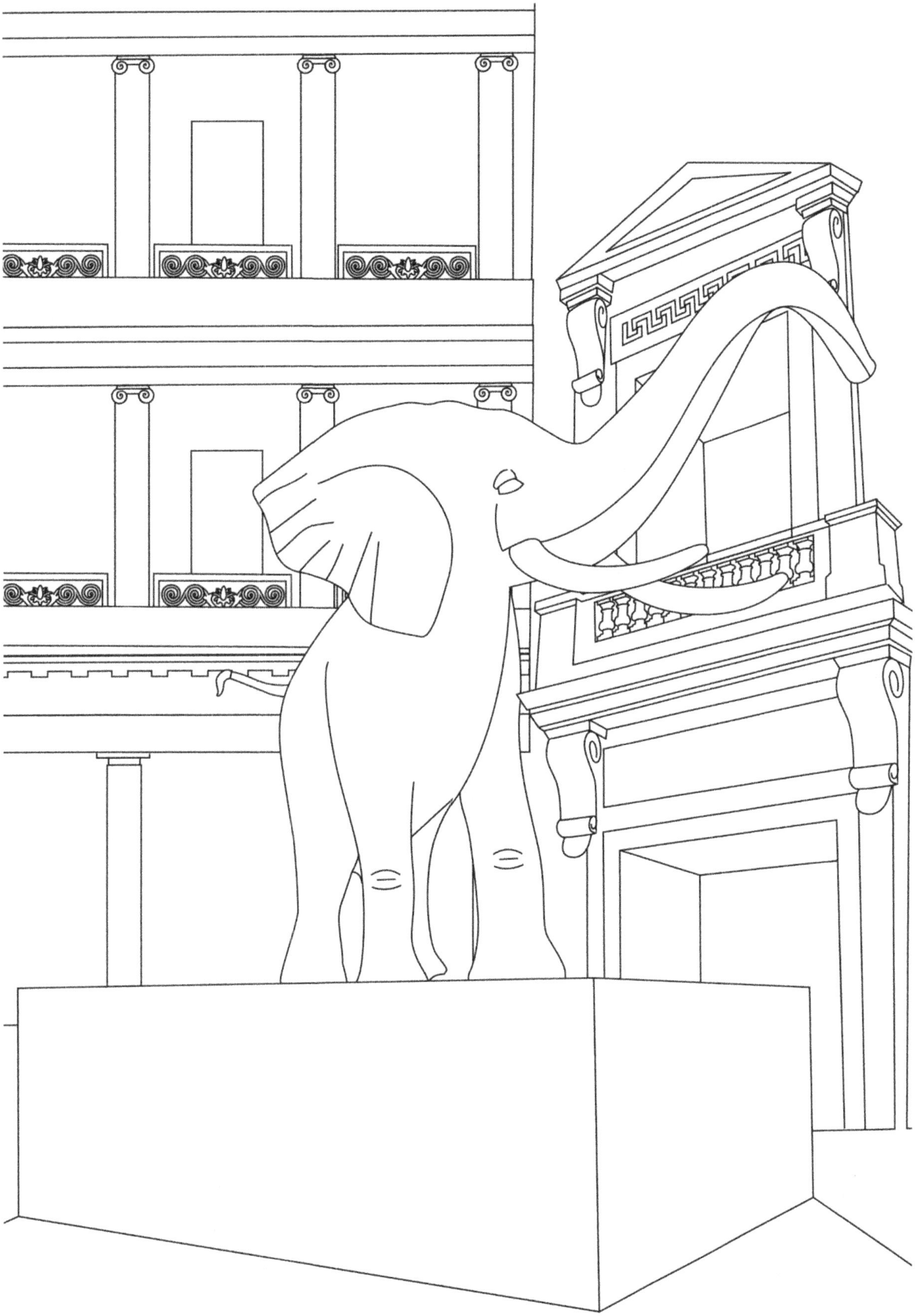

## Ford's Theater

Ford's Theater is a historic, operating theater in Washington DC. There have been plays in the theater since the 1860's. It is also the site of the assassination of President Abraham Lincoln on April 14, 1865.

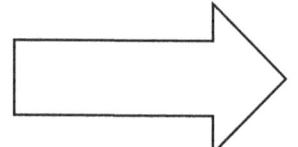

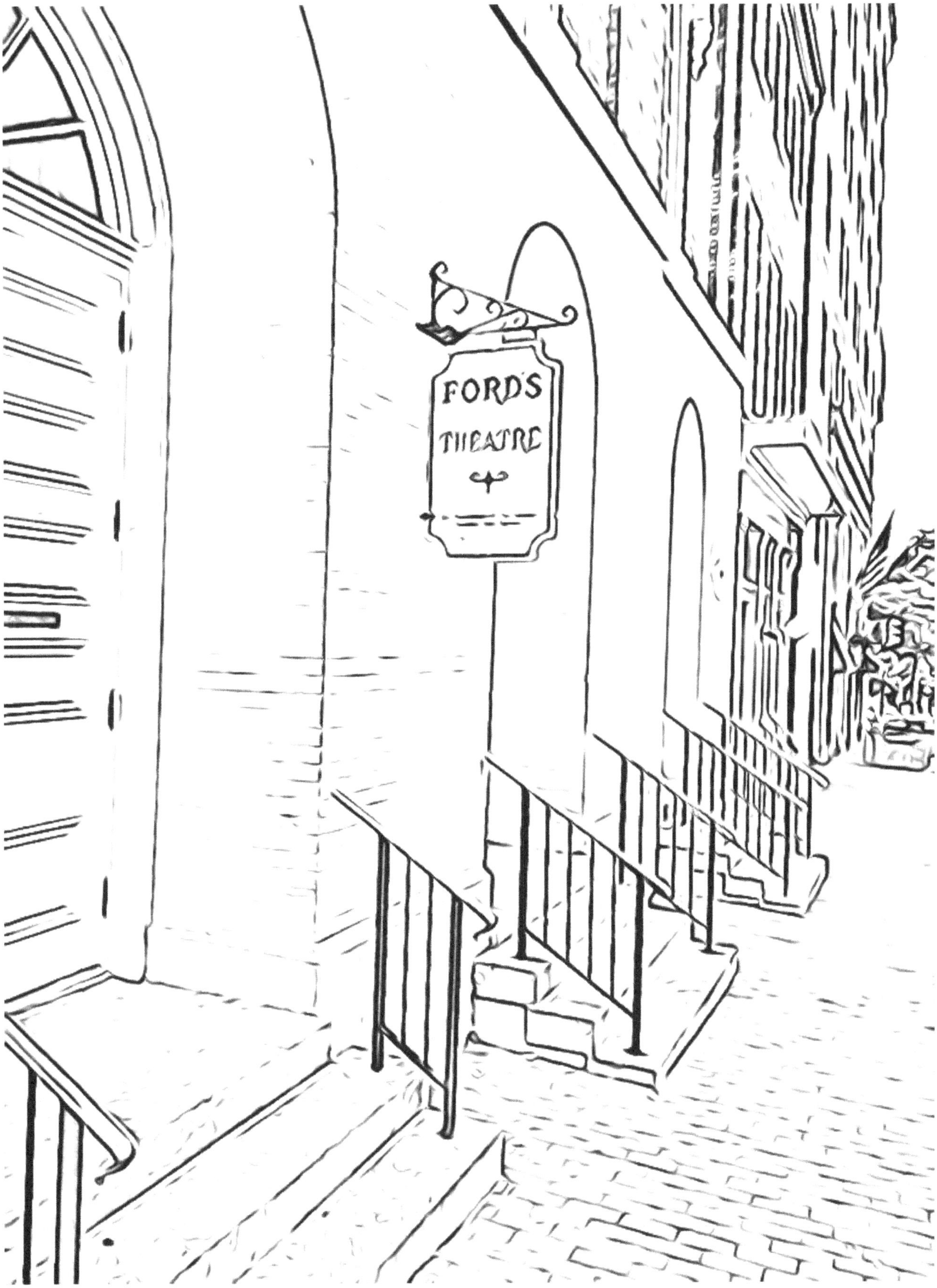
FORD'S
THEATRE

## National Zoo

Formally named The National Zoological Park, The National Zoo in Washington DC is a part of the Smithsonian Institute. This zoo is one of the oldest zoos in the United States! The panda exhibit at the zoo is called the "Great Panda Habitat"!

## National Zoo

The gorillas in the "Great Ape House" are very personable as well. The gorillas, like the one in the picture, like to watch the visitors to the zoo and sometimes make fun of them. It is fun to watch.

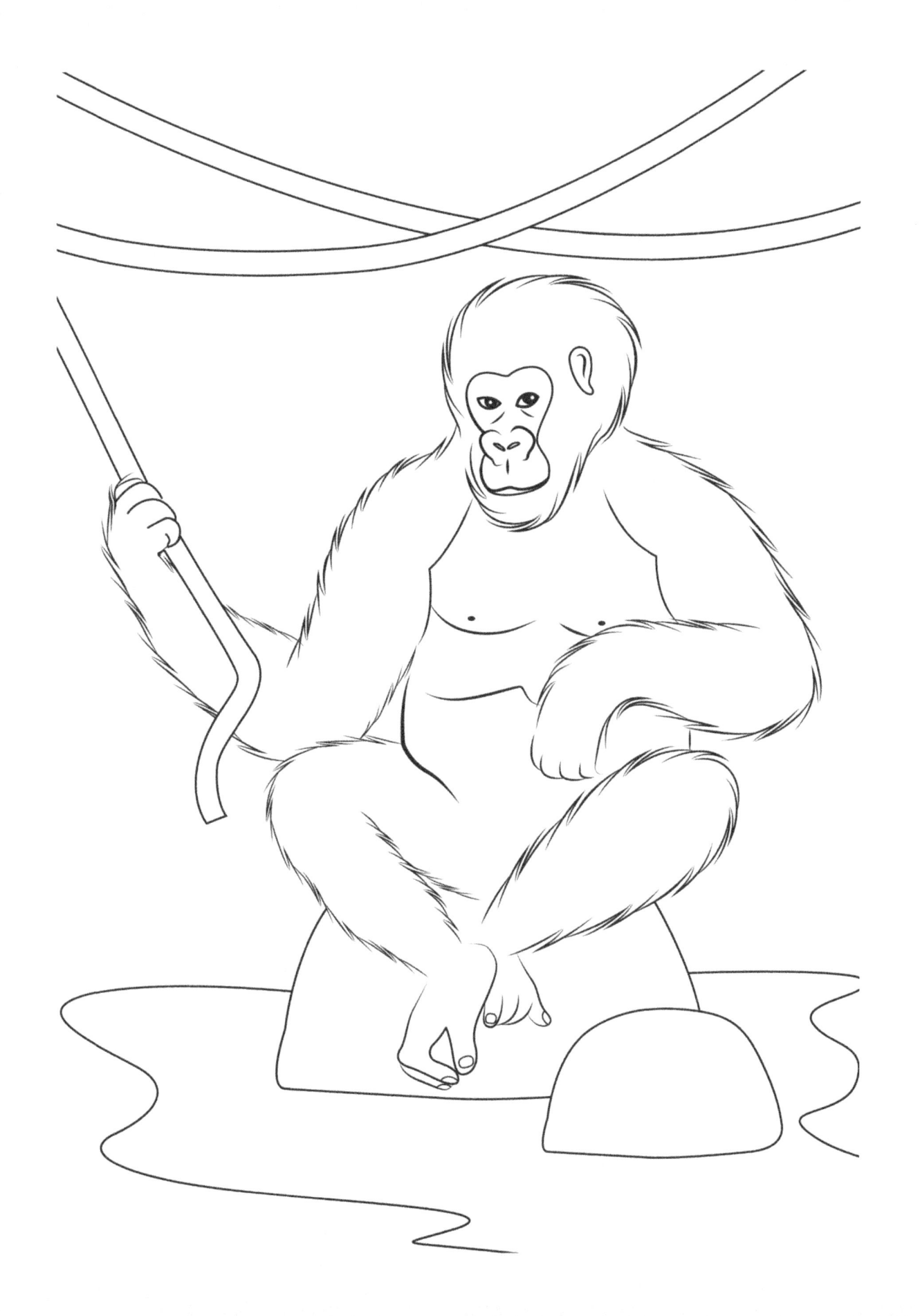

# SOLUTIONS

# Solutions

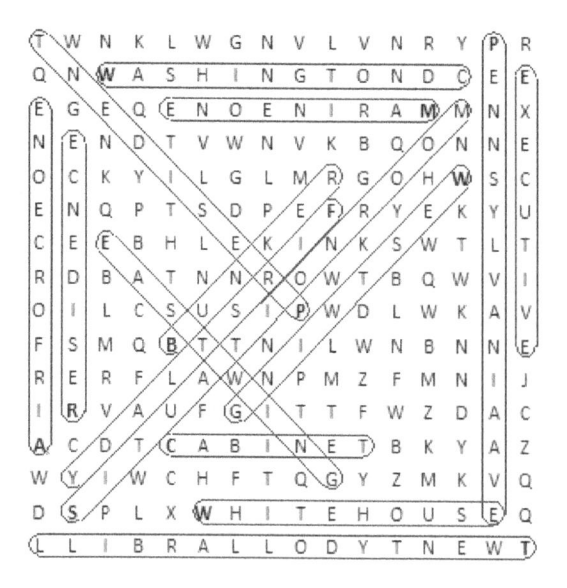

**Anagrams**
White House
monuments
washington
national zoo
washington monument
lincoln memorial
air and space museum
National Mall
fords theater
US Capitol

The reflecting pool is actually called the Lincoln Memorial Reflecting Pool and spans most of the distance between the Lincoln Memorial and the Washington Monument

# Solutions

**Word Count**
(Here are some possible words – there are more I'm sure)

Saw, was, ditch, snow, now, own, one, width, song, down, Itch, chat, tag, hang, go, hog, gnat, than, got, inch, gnaw, gown, twin, wing, twig, hand

# SOLUTIONS

**Coin Match Game**
1-E, 2-D, 3-A, 4-F, 5-C, 6-B

**Bill Match Game**
1-D, 2-B, 3-F, 4-A, 5-E, 6-G, 7-C

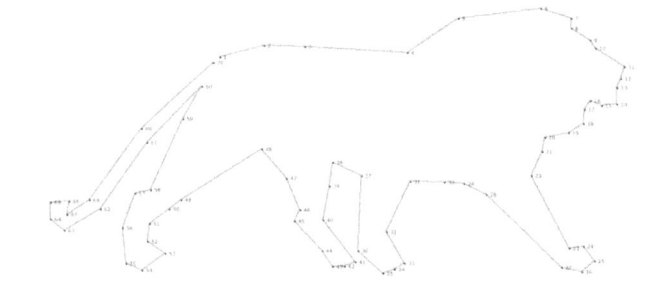

**Decode the message – Page 19**
President Abraham Lincoln was assassinated at Fords Theater

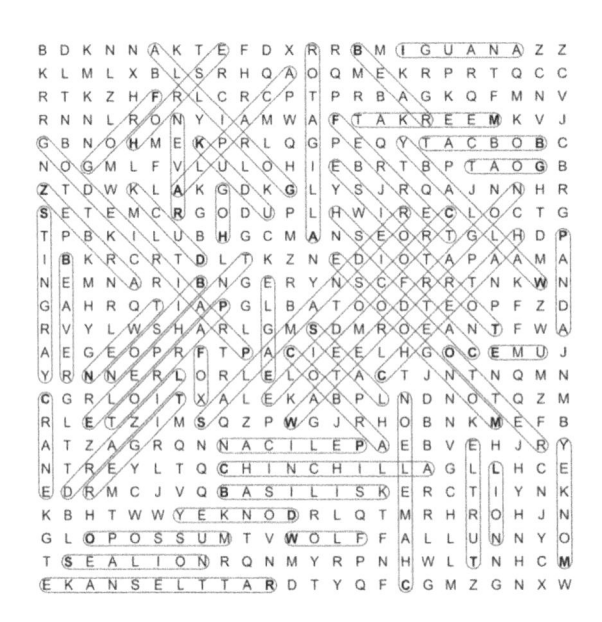

I hope this book helped make your trip to Washington DC or your trip planning more fun!

Complementary travel journal
with activity and coloring pages to
## Hey Kids! Let's Visit Washington DC

Hey Kids! Let's Visit Washington DC on amazon
https://kid-friendly-family-vacations.com/letsvisitwdc

When you take your family trip to Washington DC, I have a free gift for you!

http://kid-friendly-family-vacations.com/wdcjournal

The Hey Kids! Let's Visit series also includes visits to:

A Cruise Ship
New York City
London, England
San Francisco
Savannah, Georgia
Paris, France
Charleston, South Carolina

I hope you will join us for another visit soon!
Teresa Mills

Made in United States
North Haven, CT
07 May 2022